The Pocket Guide
to the

NEW PARADIGM

Are You Ready for the Shift?

Zia Eubanks

The Pocket Guide
to the

NEW PARADIGM

"The secret of change is to focus all your energy, not on fighting the old, but on building the new."

- Socrates

Dedication

This book is dedicated to you, the person reading these words. My hope is that you may read something in this little book that opens your heart to the truth of who you are; a magnificent, unique, one-of-a-kind expression of the divine having a human experience. Within your heart is the key to your heart's greatest desires. Not desires on the physical plane but the calling of your Soul. All of us have something that is aching to express – art, science, being a healer, a love of animals or children, writing or creating some fabulous meal and dessert. It is limitless. No matter what it might be, now is the time to honor it and nurture it to unfold. Your gifts are needed more than ever before! What could be better than a world full of people living their souls purpose filled with passion?

Together, one person at a time, waking up to the truth that lies within our hearts and beginning to live it *will* change the world!

It's time to live your Divine Design!

Contents

Introduction

What is a Paradigm?

From The American Heritage® Dictionary

paradigm
păr′ə-dīm″, -dĭm″

noun

1.   One that serves as a pattern or model.

2.   A set of assumptions, concepts, values, and practices that constitutes a way of viewing reality for the community that shares them, especially in an intellectual discipline.

In this book, the concept of paradigm is most closely aligned with this definition. It refers to a commonly held belief (consciousness) that is accepted by the majority of people.

Like a fish in a fishbowl, it is nearly impossible for it to imagine life outside the bowl, when in fact there is a vast world out there. We are all in our own fishbowl, continuing to live in a developed reality that we all unconsciously agree to call our world. This is a paradigm.

When we see things differently and start to look inward to our own innate truth, we begin to shift our perception of reality and open ourselves to the possibilities of something new. We begin to create a new set of assumptions, concepts, values, and practices. In doing so, our outer world begins to shift, and life begins to change.

The key is understanding that a paradigm is a fluid thing. It is a collective consciousness that lives and breathes. It is a shared state of being that can be altered by those engaged with it.

In this book, the ideas for a New Paradigm are being introduced and explored.

Expanded consciousness.

We Have Come to a Crossroads

The Crossroads

The last two years have been a wild time! It is a time of great transition and we have come to a crossroads. We have two choices, we can either stay connected to the current paradigm or choose to follow a new road. For years people have been talking about a "shift." Back in 2012 there was much speculation about the end of the Mayan calendar and how that would affect our modern world. Although it seemed anticlimactic at the time, the shift was already in motion. Others talk about the change of the astrological age from Pisces to Aquarius. This transition opens the return of the feminine influence, along with many other concepts. One way or another, it's becoming more and more clear that a shift is taking place.

Then along came 2020. None of us expected the changes we began seeing in our world. This is not how anyone anticipated the shift would play out, yet here it is!

So many people are awakening. They are seeing things differently than we ever have before. Many are confused and wondering what to think and whom to believe. This unexpected shift is calling us all to stop looking outside ourselves for answers and shift our perspective – to look inward to our innate Truth; to our own hearts, where our deeper understanding lies.

This is the beginning of a new era.

There is no going back to "normal."

We are all faced with a decision.

Are you going to choose

THAT WAY

or

THIS WAY

THAT WAY

The Old Paradigm

The Old Paradigm is the well-worn path. It is the road we have been on for generations. It is the same road our parents, our grandparents, and our great-grandparents have traveled. It was a good road at the beginning. It opened opportunities and lots of possibilities. Our focus changed from one of survival to having more leisurely time and discretionary money. We were taught to look outside ourselves for happiness – always seeking that "thing" that would bring us joy. We were taught to set goals, strive for success, and someday retire and enjoy our golden years. Capitalism reigned.

We learned to think that we are separate, and that having a strong ego identity is good. The world is seen in dualities: right/wrong, good/bad, Democrat/Republican, black/white, rich/poor, educated/uneducated, etc.

We learn to be competitive from an early age. It begins in school, striving for high grades, or winning in athletics, and this continues into adulthood. Jobs, cars, homes. . . keeping up with the Joneses.

Let's explore the pillars of the old paradigm.

Duality Consciousness

Duality consciousness creates a sense of separateness. We are taught to see ourselves as separate from others, and we enjoy being separate. It is satisfying to our ego.

We identify by gender, race, nationality. And within those we identify as other things that create duality as well. For example, being a Democrat or a Republican.

We are taught to see things as "good or bad", "right or wrong". Everything in our world has two sides – dark and light, up and down, left and right, back and front.

I "like" it or I "don't" like it. Neutrality is seen as indecisive.

We are deeply connected to our physicality and the 3D world of form.

All this keeps us separate, feeling isolated and alone. It is part of being human to experience duality, that is what makes up this 3D physical world. However, that is only a small part of our existence – that is part of the illusion.

The illusion is perpetuated by following the Newtonian model of physics – where we focus on matter. In the Newtonian model, science has spotlighted the physical matter and how it functions in the world. It narrows our focus on what we can see and considers the rest just empty "space".

This focus on the dense matter and the duality that is required to hold that reality is limiting us all. Although science has made a multitude of discoveries in the 20th century in the field of Quantum Physics, the old model still persists.

There is a benefit in keeping us stuck in duality. The benefit is not for us but for the current model that values profit over people.

Consumerism

In the Old Paradigm we are all seen as "consumers". Capitalism has reached a peak of greed and has transformed people into consumers at the expense of our humanity.

Corporations have more power than people, and their only concern is profit. Compassion is viewed as "emotionality" and not good for the "bottom line".

Our political system has been compromised by the influence of big money (corporations), and politicians act more often on behalf of their 'sponsors' than they do their constituents. The consumer culture belief is "what's good for 'big business' is good for the whole".

That consumer culture has shifted so dramatically that we even self-identify as "consumers" and take some pride in it. It creates a feeling of power, when in reality we are being manipulated in every way.

Seeking things outside ourselves – material things – is promoted in every aspect of our world. That external focus keeps us in a hamster wheel seeking happiness in things. When one item has lost its luster, we are off seeking the next thing.

The student loan situation is an example of the training ground. Young people are already deep in debt before they even begin their adult life. They are limited in their choices because the debt must be repaid and that becomes the priority. This sets them up for a lifetime of following the consumer model.

That reminds me of a bumper sticker I saw years ago. "I owe, I owe, so off to work I go", it read. It is funny, but it is also very true. The customer culture grooms us, ever so subtly, into that belief and behavior. It has become the accepted norm. "I owe, I owe, so off to work I go" keeps the system running.

Fear, Lack, Competition

Fear and lack are the foundation of the Old Paradigm. Scarcity and feeling like there is not enough are the hallmarks of living an externally focused paradigm. We are taught from an early age that what we want is "out there" and we proceed to seek it. Believing that acquiring it will bring us some sense of value. Yet, we worry that other people might get it before us or that others are more deserving than us. We are seeking happiness in stuff.

Competition is built into our lives from the beginning. School is where it becomes a reality for most of us. As adults we vie for positions, status, a nicer car, a bigger house, etc.

We identify "enemies", and this distinction creates an "US vs THEM" fear-based consciousness. This also justifies outrageous military spending.

All these factors keep us focused externally – looking outside ourselves for our emotional needs. When we are in fear, we seek security. When we feel a sense of lack, we seek a means to fill the void. When we are in a competitive mode, we are focused on achieving and de-emphasizing our innate nature which is more about cooperation and community.

In today's world fear is running wild. Fear can take on a life of its own, causing us a society to shift our entire focus. That is what has happened over the past two years. Fear has caused us more separation and made us question other people in a way that is damaging our sense of humanity. The Old Paradigm is beginning to collapse because of it.

We cannot sustain a healthy culture when fear, lack and competition reign. Again, this state of being is benefiting something bigger. Not us. Keeping people feeling separate with the primary emotions being fear, lack and competition allows all of us to feel uncertain, confused and in the long run more easily manipulated. We are not seeing clearly.

Identify as Form (3D)

We identify as a body. The matter of our physical form is the focus of our life. We treat our bodies as the entirety of our experience.

The medical world looks at the body in pieces and parts and rarely sees an issue beyond the single "problem" component.

We are taught to be at war with our bodies, especially women and girls. Body image and the fixation with weight and size preoccupies a vast majority of the population. Men and boys are taught to focus on strength, endurance, and being tough, ignoring their emotions.

When we identify as form, we disconnect from our deeper wisdom – our intuition.

We see the world as three dimensional and move our physical form through time and space on the material plane in a linear way. We live by Newtonian Physics.

As I explained earlier, Newtonian Physics focuses on the seen – the physical matter. This keeps us focused on the limited nature of our earthly experience. In reality, we are layers of energy coalesced into form. In the 3D world we only focus on the form.

This viewpoint is very limiting and keeps us stuck in the Old Paradigm. It ignores things that can't be explained, like our sixth sense. Most of us have experienced some type of awareness that we would call intuition or gut feelings. That is as much a part of us as the physical, but we are taught to see it as "supernatural".

There is so much that cannot be explained by Newtonian Physics that is being explained by Quantum Physics. It is the difference between focusing on the seen or on both the seen and unseen (physical and energetic). These sound like big concepts but really are quite simple at their basic understanding. In the Old Paradigm the 3D world of the seen is our primary focus.

Authoritarian God

In the Old Paradigm, God is seen as an authority figure who guides us in living a "good life".

Religion was created as a formal system to teach ideals of God and how to live accordingly.

We learn if you are good you go to "heaven" and if you are bad you go to "hell". For many people God is seen as a "Santa" type figure – watching over us and knowing when we are good or bad.

A lot of us have grown up believing that God is "a loving God" but can also be judgmental and punishing. With rules and dogma that can stifle living life. In the Old Paradigm, God is most often connected to religion.

Many people have shifted from being "religious" to being "spiritual" and have begun to find a deeper personal connection to God. However, it is most often based on a reaction to old beliefs steeped in religion.

Years ago, during my family genealogy pursuits, I discovered my 8th great-grandfather, Thomas Eubanks. He was a Quaker and came to the New World so he can openly follow his beliefs. He would have been jailed or executed because of his beliefs in the Old World. His goal was to find a place to live where he could practice his beliefs which were based on his individual relationship with God. Not intermediaries. That was in the 1640's.

Unfortunately, those Puritan beliefs he left behind found their way back, although in a less severe fashion. The Authoritarian God of the Old Paradigm creates a separation and hierarchy that keeps us believing that God (or whatever you want to call that power) is outside of us. Our path to knowing God comes with a set of rules that must be followed. This philosophy keeps us feeling isolated, judged, and challenged to "be" and "do" certain things to be accepted by God.

I know this is a hard one for many people. But I am describing the "paradigm" that is currently creating our reality. Not everyone believes it, but the majority do.

THIS WAY

The New Paradigm

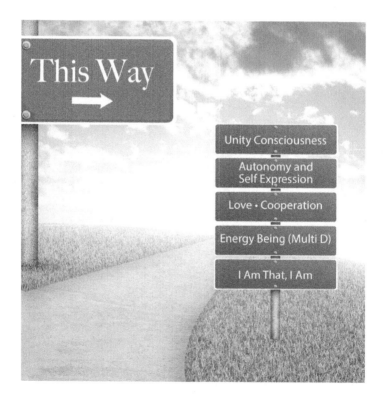

The New Paradigm is a different path. One less traveled. It is not as familiar; as a matter of fact, it is unfamiliar and filled with unknown possibilities. Behold, there is nothing to fear, these unknown and unlimited possibilities are based on a belief in love, not fear, as the reigning state (the accepted norm).

In the New Paradigm we see ourselves as multi-dimensional beings, not just the physical form. We are energy beings compressed into the physical.

Quantum physics guides the way, opening us to a universal view of living. Where the invisible is part of the equation. Vibration and frequency are vital aspects of living.

Love is the guiding principle and living a divinely heart-centered life is the path to fulfillment. Learning and following your Divine Design (purpose and authentic beingness) takes priority. We are not motivated by survival or making a living but expressing our unique gifts and working in cooperation with others to express theirs, knowing that the abundant flow is unlimited.

Let's explore the five guiding principles.

Unity Consciousness

Unity Consciousness begins with the realization that we are all connected. What we do or say effects the whole. Because we are energy beings, our energy is part of the entirety of all.

It is the understanding that everything is made of energy – the physical world that includes inanimate objects, animals, plants, rocks, *and* humans.

With a unity perspective we understand that we can trust our intuition and our gut feelings, recognizing them as a part of the Universal energy of all things. Plus, we honor and revere them as an integral part of our experience.

We live in cooperation with the flow of LIFE energy and have respect for our natural world and all of existence. We support, encourage, and work cooperatively with our fellow humans.

Although "unity" sounds like we have lost our individuality, the opposite is true. In the New Paradigm we see ourselves with autonomy as the unique expression that we are but understand that we are part of the bigger whole. It is the understanding that a wave is part of the ocean yet looks like a separate thing. We are the same, unique in our human experience, yet part of the bigger humanity.

When we shift from duality consciousness to unity consciousness, we are altering our perception and self-identification, as well as our outlook towards others. Understanding that each and every one of us is part of the bigger whole creates a consciousness of inclusion and compassion. Something that is greatly needed in our world today.

Opening to and accepting ourselves as the full spectrum of our being, knowing that what we do affects the whole, makes us behave differently. It creates an attitude of cooperation and support

Autonomy and Self Expression

The post materialism era moves us out of the collective "consumer" driven identity into one of sovereign consciousness and an elevated sense of personal self-expression. Connecting with that greater understanding at our core and owning our own Divine Design.

We respect our authentic, individual Truth and allow LOVE to guide our life. The understanding of how this connection activates the flow of abundance and prosperity is accepted and practiced. With the understanding that abundance is our divine right, there is no need to experience lack or limitation.

With autonomy and authentic self-expression, people will work cooperatively, sharing their gifts and encouraging others to express theirs. All the while knowing that in cooperation and living divinely heart-centered lives, there is enough for everyone.

Autonomy is the understanding that you are an independent being. Your true authority comes from within. In the Old Paradigm we are taught to look outwardly to authority figures for guidance. In the New Paradigm we turn within, to our own innate truths and values, ideals that are held deeply in our hearts. We have been taught to ignore these, however, in the New Paradigm they become the pillars for your life.

Part of that autonomy is your vision for your life. That includes your unique self-expression. When we can come out from under the cloud of "I owe, I owe, so off to work I go" we can step back and check in with ourselves to find our true course, the passion and Divine Design that is unique to each of us. When we take the time to look within and find that, then we live differently. Our motivation shifts from one of making money to one of expressing our particular gifts. Then the Universe rises up to support us.

Love and Cooperation

In the New Paradigm we understand that
LOVE is the center of our life experience. Learning
to live life through our heart center and through
the Truth of that knowledge.

We have been living focused on the external
world and looking for ways to protect ourselves
from pain and suffering. The new way of thinking
places our focus internally, connected to the
greater idea of ourselves as the magnificent beings
we are.

When we change our thinking in this way it
changes how we deal and relate to ourselves and
others. Love and cooperation urge us to trust in
each other and encourages each of us to see the
good in the other. Together, as we live in this

consciousness, it allows us all to live more fully in our authentic nature. Everyone is accepted and welcomed to live their unique Divine Design.

Living from a place of love sounds Pollyanna-ish to many people. It takes a deeper understanding of the BIG LOVE this book is addressing. It is the Universal Love that is the basis of the human experience. It is recognizing the good within people and the basic truth of our compassion that arises in so many situations. Everything from helping a stranger reach something on a high shelf at the grocery store to traveling to an area hit by a tornado or hurricane to help out. It is built into our nature.

That care, compassion, and cooperation acts like a catalyst for elevating our spirts, bringing people together, and building a sense of community. When we shift from living in a fear-based society to a love-based society we find ways to care and support each other. When we treat each other with this heightened sense of dignity it changes everything.

This type of love isn't sappy or naive. It is strong, fierce, and as natural as breathing.

Energy Beings (Multi D)

In the New Paradigm we identify ourselves as multi-dimensional "energy beings". When we view ourselves in that fashion, we understand that we are more than the physical. To truly heal ourselves requires the entirety of the physical, the emotional, the mental, and the energetic.

As energy beings we understand how frequency and vibration play a role in our life and we honor that wisdom.

In the New Paradigm energy medicine and energy treatments will be the norm. The science of energy will expand in ways we can't fathom today. It will no longer be called "woo woo" or "new age", it will be honored as an advanced form of human design and self-care.

When we begin to clearly see that we are energy beings, so much more than the physical body we can see and touch, it will dramatically change the quality of life on the planet.

Dr. Sue Morter writes in her book *The Energy Codes*, "We are spiritual beings having a spiritual experience at the physical end of the energy spectrum". As she describes, we are physical matter coalesced from higher levels of energy into denser and denser form. The form (our physical body) is not the whole. It is the part we can see with the naked eye, but we are much, much more.

In the New Paradigm we begin to acknowledge this truth and learn to see ourselves in a larger spectrum. We can look to ancient teachings like the Chakra system, the Chinese meridians, or the life force energy of chi as a source of wisdom that most of modern science has abandoned. There are many ancient teachings that are as relevant today as ever. When we begin to expand our consciousness to this understanding, we can heal ourselves on deeper levels – physically, emotionally, and spiritually.

I Am That I Am

In the New Paradigm the key to living life is the understanding that each of us is a unique expression of the Divine. Like a wave is part of the ocean, we are part of the Universal consciousness of all creation in an energy body. Each a one-of-a-kind, never before, never again expression of that Force.

When we understand that, we begin to live life differently. We begin to see that we have inside us all the attributes of the Divine: love, joy, peace, prosperity, creativity, unlimited self-expression. All belonging to us, expressed in a way no one else can express. In a spiritual sense we cannot be confined or defined by religion, nor do we want to be. We can participate but recognize that we are a piece of God having an experience of being human. That cannot be limited.

We also know that every other individual on the planet is that same thing. No one is better or less than another. We are all unique expressions of the ONE, all connected. It is an attitude of grace and a knowledge that there is a goodness and a greatness that runs through all.

Each person comes to understand their own unique Divine Design and learns to express it fully.

When we connect with that deeper understanding and see ourselves as the unique, magnificent beings that we are, life becomes more sacred.

When we begin to understand "I Am That I Am" and connect with our Divine nature we release limitations that had previously kept us tethered to the Old Paradigm.

This does not mean we have to abandon our connection to religion or turn our backs. It requires us to remember that our connection to our Source is primary and unique to each and every one of us. You are a piece of God having a human experience!

THIS WAY OR THAT WAY

Which way will you choose?

The decision is one we each need to make. Either way, it will be a bumpy road. As the old breaks down and the new emerges, the changes will make life seem different and even challenging. If you choose "That Way" and stick with the Old Paradigm, there will be a lot of fear and loss. As the old systems begin to unravel, it will be frightening. Clinging to the old ways, hoping that things will "return to normal", will cause a lot of stress, frustration, and anxiety. All the attributes of the Old Paradigm will be amplified and as we see now, division and separation will continue to grow. In the Old Paradigm we are manipulated by fear, and that is driven by the media and the government.

Years ago, I read a book by Daniel Pink called *A Whole New Mind*. He explained that a lot of the most creative minds in our country are working in advertising. Those creative minds are put to work by advertising agencies who are hired by huge corporations (and our government) to influence us into behaving in ways that benefit them. The statistics on how much influence they garner is mind boggling. The number of ads we are subjected to daily is astounding! Especially with the onset of social media that has grown exponentially. If you want your mind opened to the power of social media, watch the documentary *"The Social Dilemma"*.

On the other hand, if you are aware of the shift and ready to start living in the New Paradigm, then you face a different set of issues. The world as we know it is still crumbling. We will all face many of the same challenges. However, in the New Paradigm we understand that even though we can't see it, we know that good will prevail. We understand that as energy beings we can raise our vibration and our frequency, and in that invisible field the world we imagine is already on its way. There is a power and strength in this understanding that breaks through fear and separation. When we understand we have personal sovereignty and autonomy within the whole, then we are free. It is knowing that we are all connected, yet unique emanations of the Divine that we can live with hope, knowing that we are part of the great awakening on the planet.

I am choosing THIS WAY – The New Paradigm. I am making the decision to live it like it is already here. That is my call. It feels unfamiliar, but that is good. As Albert Einstein said, "We cannot solve a problem with the same thinking we used when we created them".

It's time to look at things differently. It's time to use the science of Quantum Physics as our guide – to bring the invisible to the visible. The world I described in this book is out there in the Quantum Field. All it takes is enough of us seeing it and believing in it to bring it into this reality.

It is possible.

I am off on a journey into the new paradigm!

"You never change things by fighting the existing reality. To change something build a new model that makes the existing one obsolete."

-Buckminster Fuller

Choosing THIS WAY

Simple Steps to Living the 5 Guiding Principles

If after reading this book you have chosen to head THIS WAY towards the New Paradigm, here are some ideas to get your started on your journey.

The first thing that is required is an open mind. That is easier said than done. It is our nature to be skeptical. It is also our nature to allow our ego to lead that way. Our ego has enormous power over us, and it likes all its roles and labels. Maintaining the status quo is paramount to the ego. However, to open yourself to a new way of living you must let go of the known and step out into unfamiliar territory. Dr. Joe Dispenza calls this the "river of the unknown". It is scary territory. It takes being present in the moment, understanding that neither the past nor the future have any power over you. It takes turning your focus inward and exploring your heart. What are your heart's greatest desires? Again, these are not material things but the unique heart code that makes you, YOU. It is different for every person.

Next is accepting the concept that you are a unique expression of the Divine having a human experience. Or, as Dr. Morter states, "spiritual beings having a spiritual experience at the physical end of the energy spectrum". It takes owning this concept and realizing that what God is, you are. All the attributes of the divine are your attributes. You are not broken or in need of repair. You have just forgotten. It's part of the human experience.

Let's explore the concepts of the New Paradigm further.

Guiding Principle #1: Unity Consciousness

Look at all the ways you identify yourself as different from others, whether it be a political party or even your job title. The quickest way to break out of duality consciousness is to become aware of the ways you self-identify and separate yourself from others. Many of them are very subtle. Many of them seem deeply seated in your life experience and family history. Many of them have been programmed into us from our childhood, peers, and society. However, all of them are just a belief that we hold as real. This is the key to understanding a paradigm. It is a set of assumptions, concepts, values, and practices that constitutes a way of viewing reality. In order to step out of the Old Paradigm, you must change those things. Awareness is required, you can't change what you don't look at.

During my own spiritual awakening I began to see it as "the BIG letting go". Allowing myself to let go of everything I thought I knew about my reality and me. In order to change I had to let go of old conditioned beliefs about myself and all the things I was desperately holding on to as my identity. I'm not saying it's easy, but it is liberating.

It is accepting the idea of being part of the bigger Oneness that will free you. Letting go of all the old (limiting) beliefs and opening to the possibility of something bigger will catapult you into the New Paradigm. Understanding that we are all connected in this Quantum soup and what you do affects the whole is huge. That is Unity Consciousness.

Make a list of all the ways you identify yourself. Dig deep. Be honest. Think about how this identity keeps you in the Old Paradigm. Then ask yourself which of them you are willing to let go.

Guiding Principle #2: Autonomy and Self-Expression

Autonomy is the understanding that you are a sovereign being. It is your right as a human to certain dignities. You have control and power over your body and your life. You have free will and self-determination. You control your thoughts and what goes on in your mind is private. These are not just rights as an American, these are human rights.

This is an important fact to consider. What does autonomy mean to you? Have you ever really given it any thought? Maybe you should. Take some time and write about it in your journal. We have grown so accustomed to following rules and the crowd that we are losing our sense of autonomy.

Let me point out again that autonomy and unity consciousness are not exclusive. Autonomy is your personal experience based on your unique heart code, AND you are still a part of the whole. Like the wave and ocean analogy, separate yet part of the bigger whole.

The other part of your uniqueness is your self-expression. Each of us have different interests, desires, and passions. At times we get caught up in thinking our "purpose" must be this big thing – being the next Oprah or taking the art world by storm. Sometimes, actually most times, it is far less grand. It is the simple calling of your Soul. If you take some time and think back to when you were a child and remember what it was you loved to do, it will give you some clues. Or you might know what it is that you love doing but stop yourself because it seems silly, impossible, or would upset some aspect of your life. In the New Paradigm we release all those blocks and begin to value and honor that aspect of ourselves. Uncovering what makes your heart sing and giving it a voice is paramount in this shift. Connecting with your heart and allowing what it wants to express is your assignment.

Take some time to daydream and explore what your life would look like if you allowed yourself to honestly express your passion. Write about it, or talk to your friends about it and ask them to tell you theirs. It is time for all of us to start following our hearts.

Guiding Principle #3: Love and Cooperation

The first thing you must understand about this guiding principle is that the love discussed in the book is BIG LOVE. Universal Love. It is the power and force behind everything.

When I had my first spiritual awakening as a teenager, I felt that love. I was doing a student teaching assignment at an elementary school in a second-grade classroom. One day, on the playground, the kids wanted to push *me* in the swings instead of our normal routine of me pushing them. I agreed and several of them started pushing me. They pushed harder and harder, and I was swinging high into the sky. During one intense swing I pushed my head back and my feet high and suddenly I felt like I could fly. I was being pulled by something bigger. It felt like an out of body experience. Along with this intense feeling of absolute freedom was an all-encompassing feeling of love. I felt bathed in it, absorbed in it. It felt better than anything I had ever experienced. Honestly, I can still remember that feeling today.

In the New Paradigm we must come to understand this Universal Love. It is the force behind everything! When we connect with this powerful state, we shift our way of thinking and release judgement. Judgement of ourselves and others. We begin to hold a benevolence within our hearts that leads to a new way of being. Cooperation and support of others becomes a natural activity.

Take some time to contemplate this idea. Journal about it. Write down any experiences you have had with Universal Love. It comes in millions of variations.

Begin a meditation practice. Quiet your mind and open your heart. Allow yourself to go into the empty space of the unknown and see what happens.

Guiding Principle #4: Energy Beings (Multi D)

This guiding principle asks you to see yourself as more than your physical being. This one requires an open mind again. Accepting and realizing that you are an energy being means recognizing that you are bigger than your physical body.

One day I was listening to a podcast and the person talked about the energy of your thoughts. He said the energy of a thought goes out of your head and into the ether. It made me wonder how far it could travel. Does the energy of my thought just float around me like a personal cloud? That's when I began imaging the Quantum field. It made me realize that this was part of the Law of Attraction. When I send out a thought (energy) it goes out into the field and finds similar energy – like attracts like. The statement "Thoughts Create Reality" seemed way more meaningful to me after that. Although I can't see my thought, it is actively creating my life.

The auric field is the energy field around our body. It is said to have seven layers that are correspond to the seven chakras – Etheric, Emotional, Mental, Astral, Etheric Template, Celestial, and Causal. It is this field that allows us to get a "vibe" from someone or someplace. Everything has a field; it is the nature of energy.

To harmonize and balance these fields takes an understanding of vibration and frequency. In David Hawkins' book, *Power vs Force,* he describes different emotions and their effect on our energy field. His chart has feelings like shame, guilt, fear at the low end of the spectrum, and love, joy, enlightenment at the top. In the New Paradigm we are being called to raise our vibration. Doing that requires moving out of the lower frequencies and into the higher ones. That takes a conscious effort. In our world today it is easy to get sucked down into the lower frequencies. All you have to do is watch the news!

A simple way to begin understanding this principle is to pay attention to your feelings. Go on the internet and do a search for "Power vs Force Scale". Print it out and start observing your reactions to things. Another great way to learn more about your energy body is to read Dr.

Morter's book, *The Energy Codes,* or watch her on Gaia TV. There is so much to discover about being an energy being. Start doing some research. There are hundreds of resources.

Guiding Principle #5:
I Am That I Am

As above, so below

Most of us have heard or read that quote. It originates from the Emerald Tablets. The phrase expresses the concept of microcosm and macrocosm: that smaller systems – particularly the human body – are a miniature version of the larger universe. This idea is thousands of years old.

This concept is the foundation behind Guiding Principle #5 – I Am That I Am. Recognizing that you are the microcosm of the bigger macrocosm. Whatever you believe it to be, you are a part of the bigger whole.

For years I have followed Rev. Dr. Michael Bernard Beckwith. One of his favorite sayings is, "You are a unique emanation of the Divine". After hearing this for years, one day I decided to look up the word "emanation". I went to the Merriam-

Webster Dictionary online and found this definition: "the origination of the world by a series of hierarchically descending radiations from the Godhead through intermediate stages to matter". Wow! Honestly, at first it made me laugh. It took a while for me to get my head around it, but then I got it. I Am That I Am. What the Universe is I am, just in a micro form. My micro form looks like a human woman.

We live in a holographic world on a multitude of levels. The interesting thing about a hologram is that no matter how many pieces you cut it into it still holds the original in every aspect. That is the idea that Principle #5 is teaching. We are all part of something so much bigger than we can even comprehend. We have limited ourselves by the narrow focus of matter – our physical reality. In truth, we are limitless. We hold within us the creative powers of the Universe.

It is a well-known concept that we only use a small percentage of our brain's ability, some say less than 10%. What if we expanded our consciousness and used more of the mysterious abilities of the 90%?

Deep within our brain is our pineal gland. It has been discovered that this little cone-shaped gland contains crystals. How interesting is that? Crystals are a conduit for energy and frequency, like in a transistor radio or a television receiver. Is it any wonder this area of the body is called the Third Eye in the Chakra system? Is this little gland an instrument that we have forgotten how to use?

Could these things be part of our connection to higher realms and understanding our connection to "As above, so below"?

To begin to understand this principle, take some time and contemplate what you just read. How does that resonate with you? How would your worldview shift if you believed this to be true? What if we learned to access the other 90% of our brain and tapped into the abilities of our pineal gland? This is a big concept. Take your time and process the possibilities.

* * *

These suggestions are just a brief glimpse into the New Paradigm. Once you begin to open yourself to the concepts you will begin to see your world open up. You will hear things differently, see things you didn't notice before, and people and situations come into your life unexpectedly. A quote I have lived by for years is from Dr. Wayne Dyer, "Keep a mind that is open to everything and attached to nothing". When you walk through life with an open mind, releasing judgement, it changes the way you see things. When you change the way you look at things, the things you look at change. When you release your attachments to old beliefs and conditioning, you are free to experience life in a new way. There is a freedom in this way of being that can transform your life.

Blessing to you on the journey. Thank you for bringing your energy to this new idea. Together we can shift the world into the New Paradigm.

Where Did These Ideas Come From?

This information came to me in early 2020 during a meditation. I had been meditating regularly and going deeper and deeper. On this particular day I went especially deep and was shown the information as I have laid it out here. I saw the sign "This Way or That Way" and the two roads. I was shown what it looked like on both paths. When I came out of the meditation, I went directly to my whiteboard and started writing out the ideas and thoughts that came to me during the meditation. I fully understand that this information was a "download" from the field. I'm not sure why it came to me, but I do know that I am being called to share this information about the New Paradigm. For the longest time I have held back sharing this, feeling that it was presumptuous of me to think that I know anything about what this "shift" is all about or define it in any way. However, as time has passed and more and more of the Old Paradigm is degrading, I clearly see that I must share this information. I realize that it would be an injustice to the world to hold back what Universal consciousness has bestowed upon me.

So, this is the beginning. I have already started to expand the concepts and I am compiling ideas for each of the 5 Guiding Principles to explain them in a more tangible and complete way.

As I have learned, on many levels, where attention goes, energy follows. That is why I have made the decision to begin living these beliefs in my own life. Although it may be challenging and require an entirely new mindset, I'm going for it. I feel that if I am going to teach it, I *must* live it! The more attention I give to it the more it will become my reality.

"Remember, whatever we put our attention on expands in our experience, so consider where you are focusing your time and energy."

-Deepak Chopra

Gratitude

Thank you for reading The Pocket Guide to the New Paradigm. I hope it gave you some new ideas to consider. I am grateful for you and honored to have you read my words and the concepts that I have presented.

I've made up my mind and have decided to choose THIS WAY. I am heading into the New Paradigm and will begin living life with the 5 Guiding Principles as my guideposts. As with anything new it feels a bit awkward and unfamiliar. That is why I am jumping in with both feet! I've lived my life in the Old Paradigm and much of it feels like the real me, but I now understand it is actually learned behavior through programming and repetition. The saying "You can't teach an old dog new tricks" seems applicable, but is unequivocally false. Change is the only constant in our lives. So again, I am jumping in to begin creating something new and more aligned with my Soul.

The other thing I know is that life is ever unfolding. Just like anything in nature, we are in the constant state of unfolding, and even more so when our Divine Design gets activated. Mine is getting activated as a creator and teacher. These attributes have always been part of me, but since my "big" spiritual awakening in 2016 I've realized the focus has been narrowed. Now here I am seeing myself as a creator and teacher for the New Paradigm. Life is definitely interesting!

I've decided to share my journey. I'm not exactly sure how that is going to look at the moment. You can follow me on Facebook @ZiaEubanks and on Instagram @GottaCre8.

I have included an infographic describing the 5 Guiding Principles of the New Paradigm on the next page.

Love and Blessing,

Zia

Old Paradigm	New Paradigm

Duality Consciousness

- We are separate
- We enjoy that identification
- Gender, race, nationality, party
- Focus on opposites

Unity Consciousness

- We are all connected
- What we do effects the whole
- One with everything
- We are energy

Consumerism

- Capitalism rules
- Identify as "consumer"
- Corps more powerful than people
- Politics influenced by corps

Autonomy • Self-Expression

- We are Sovereign beings
- Universal flow - always enough
- Individual Truth & Design
- Ultimate authority is self

Fear • Competition

- Fear, lack, scarcity consciousness
- External focus
- Winning, attaining before others
- Us vs Them mentality

Love • Cooperation

- Love is center of Life
- Internal focus on "being"
- Natural inclination - innate
- Cooperation & compassion

Physical Being (3D)

- Identify as a body
- Medicine treats "parts"
- Time & space - linear
- Newtonian physics

Energy Being (Multi-D)

- Multi-dimensional energy being
- Identify as layers of energy
- Connected to frequency & vibes
- Healing all levels - energy medicine
- Quantum physics

Authoritarian God

- God governs with rules
- Heaven and Hell
- Religion teaches about God
- There is a hierarchy to connect

I Am That, I Am

- We are each unique expressions
- Never before, never again
- Poses all attributes of the Divine
- Individual relationship with God

New Paradigm Guide: The 5 Guiding Principles

Zia Eubanks © 2021

Glossary of Terms

Below is a glossary of terms to help explain and define some of the words I use. These are my definitions and how they have meaning in the context of this book.

AUTONOMY:
Autonomy is a person's ability to act on his or her own values, interests, and passions. It requires a sense of self-worth and self-respect.

BEINGNESS:
This term refers to the understanding that we are spiritual beings experiencing life as a physical human. When we embrace that fact, we embody our "beingness" and live life from a perspective of the spirit, not our physical form. Being the "being" we are created as an eternal being.

DIVINE:
The Divine is the power and force from the Universe that runs through us and all things – the God essence. The Divine is the common thread of our existence.

DIVINE DESIGN:
Each of us is a unique expression of the Divine experiencing life as a physical human. Born within us is the Divine Design for our lives. Some call it "purpose", others call it "our authentic self". In

this Guide we consider it the foundation of your life experience. Many people are unaware of their purpose, authentic self, and Divine Design and are seeking that understanding. This guide is a way to discover it.

ENERGY BODY:
The energy body is that part of us that can't be seen with the human eye. Many people know about the seven energy centers of the Chakra system or the Chinese Meridians system that follows the life-energy flow of Qi in the body. These systems work with the energy body. There are different levels: physical, etherical, emotional, mental, and spiritual.

FLOW:
The Universal Flow is the invisible field of energy that runs through all things, just like a river. We can connect to the flow and experience ease. Or we can resist the flow and experience struggle, like trying to paddle upstream. The Flow allows more serenity in living and connects us with all attributes of the Divine.

FORCE:
Force with a capital "F" refers to the Universal flow. It stems from the origins of the cosmos during the Big Bang that started it all. There is a force that runs through everything that is always expanding. We are part of this expansion and also

part of the energy that it contains. We have this Force within us and it connects us to the flow.

HEART CENTERED:
Heart centered refers to living this human experience guided by the spark of the Divine instilled in your heart center. The idea is to recognize, connect with, and follow the innate wisdom of your heart.

LIFE ENERGY:
Life Energy is the energy built into our physical body through our spirit. It flows through us, as us, and can be increased or decreased. As a being with free will and a thinking mind, we can change the flow by our frequency and vibration, which are controlled by our heart, mind, and emotions.

MULTI-DIMENSONAL:
An understanding that we are more than what we see in the material world. Our physical bodies exist in a three-dimensional world, but we are much more than what we can see with our human eyes. There are a variety of beliefs about what the other dimensions entail and includes different levels and parallel realities. What this guide proposes is that we open our minds to the "idea" of being multi-dimensional beings and how that can shift our reality.

ONE:

The ONE is a reference to the oneness that connects us all. It is the flow of the Universe that connects everything – person, place, or thing. We can call it God, Source, Universe, or Quantum Field, etc.

PARADIGM: A shared set of beliefs that create a reality that a group of people agree as true. This is a collective consciousness that creates the reality they all share. A paradigm shift is when the collective consciousness changes, which in turn changes reality as it was previously known. Paradigms are fluid.

QUANTUM PHYSICS:

Quantum physics is the study of matter and energy at its most fundamental level. A central tenet of quantum physics is that energy comes in indivisible packets called quanta. Quantum Physics changes the way we look at the world and is a new perspective on science — quite different than the Old Paradigm where Newtonian physics focuses only on matter. The Quantum Field is the entirety of a cell, not just the physical matter. The field that is 5% visible matter and 95% invisible — where infinite possibilities reside.

SOVEREIGN:

Sovereign in the guide refers to personal authority. We are sovereign beings that have sole responsibility and decision making over our own bodies and lives. It is the foundation of our free will.

TRUTH:

Truth with a capital "T" refers to our internal Truth. That gut level knowledge of what is right or wrong for you as an individual. It is a deep connection to your own divinity and what makes you the unique expression that you are. The goal of the New Paradigm is for each of us to uncover and live our own Truth. To live our unique Divine Design!

Other books by Zia Eubanks

Becoming Zia: A Tale of Transformation

Becoming You! Interactive Workbook

God Cards: Exploring the Seven Aspects of God

A Kid from Akron, Ohio's Vietnam Story:
A Journey from Innocence to Mental Illness

"The world we are experiencing today is the result of our collective consciousness, and if we want a new world, each of us must start taking responsibility for helping create it."

-Rosemary Fillmore Rhea

About the Author

Zia Eubanks is a writer, spiritual seeker and visionary. Her first spiritual awakening came in her teens when she accidentally connected with the ONENESS. This experience allowed her to feel the bigger love that exists in the field and opened her to the idea of something greater.

She has been actively seeking a deeper sense of connection and understanding of elevated consciousness for nearly 30 years.

This book is the result of a "download" during a deep meditation. Using her creative nature and writing skills, she created this pocket guide. Currently she is printing copies of this book and plans on distributing them on her travels for free because she wants the information to be shared.

In this time of great change on the planet, we are all being called to express our unique gifts. Zia feels she is being called to share these ideas and is currently working other projects to delve deeper into the principles shared in this booklet.

Zia was greatly influenced by the understanding that we are all creators. It is her belief that each and every person needs to open up to their true nature and begin to live their own unique Divine Design.

> "We are all artists. Our life is our greatest creation."
>
> - Zia Eubanks

Living from that point of view, and the understanding that we are spiritual beings having a human experience, guides her life.

Zia lives in the mountains of Arizona with her partner Larry and their little dog Dixie.

Connect with Zia

Facebook @ZiaEubanks

Instagram @GottaCre8

admin@gottacre8.com

Amazon Authors page:
https://amazon.com/author/ziaeubanks

Notes

Made in the USA
Middletown, DE
02 July 2022

67963381R00050